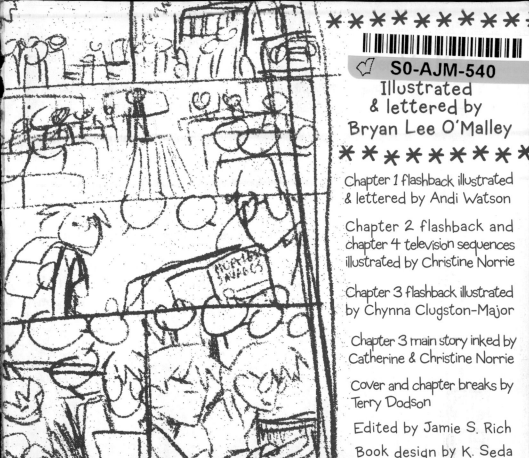

Illustrated
& lettered by
Bryan Lee O'Malley

Chapter 1 flashback illustrated
& lettered by Andi Watson

Chapter 2 flashback and
chapter 4 television sequences
illustrated by Christine Norrie

Chapter 3 flashback illustrated
by Chynna Clugston-Major

Chapter 3 main story inked by
Catherine & Christine Norrie

Cover and chapter breaks by
Terry Dodson

Edited by Jamie S. Rich

Book design by K. Seda

HOPELESS SAVAGES

Ground Zero

Hopeless Savages logo based on a logo designed by
Andi Watson

Chapter 2 flashback, chapter 4 television sequences lettered by
Spookoo (Christine Norrie, Matty Ryan, & Andrew Lis)

Chapter 3 flashback lettered by
Bryan Lee O'Malley

Published by Oni Press, Inc.
Joe Nozemack, publisher
Jamie S. Rich, editor in chief
James Lucas Jones, associate editor

This book collects all four issues of the Oni Press comic
book series Hopeless Savages: Ground Zero.

ONI PRESS, INC.
6336 SE Milwaukie Avenue, PMB30
Portland, OR 97202
USA

www.onipress.com
www.spookoo.com

First Oni Press edition: March 2003
ISBN 1-929998-52-X

1 3 5 7 9 10 8 6 4 2
PRINTED IN CANADA.

There aren't a lot of good songs about superheroes.

There's "Waiting For Superman" by The Flaming Lips, "Ghostrider" by the Henry Rollins Band, and...well, that's pretty much it, unless you're a fan of "Magneto and Titanium Man" by Wings, or "Captain America" by Jimmy Buffet.

♥INTRODUCTION♥

It's therefore perhaps only right and proper that there are so few good comics about love. It's the cultural exchange programme that never was. Pop music doesn't get to have any great adolescent power fantasies (well, apart from the one about being rock music), and comics don't get to express the mysteries of the human heart. Sure, there are lots of comics about relationships, and even a few that flirt with subtler emotions than "grrr" and "argh," but love? Romance comics died out in the '50s.

Which makes *Hopeless Savages* either a glorious throwback, or the first of some strange new hyphenated sub-genre, like retro-post-romantic comics lit. Or, it just is what it is, and what it is is something incredibly rare: a really great comic about love.

It must be rare, because frankly, I hate love, and I love this comic.

I am, of course, single. I resent all couples, with their constant inseparability and their cutesy insufferability. I detest their snuggling and their moony-eyed staring and their banal chitter-chatter. And most of all, I bitterly resent their ability to find happiness in the arms of another. Damn them.

As I write this, it's mere days away from Valentine's Day, so my dander is up. The TV is full of ads for Greatest Love Song compilations that can drain the soul and destroy any right thinking man's faith in humanity. The track listings mix in bona fide classics by Marvin Gaye and Carole King with Celine Dion's "Think Twice" and Michael Bolton's "How Am I Supposed To Live Without You." The most offensive thing being, to some people, Michael Bolton and Celine Dion really do speak of love. Because if you're in love, even Mariah Carey seems passionate and sincere.

Any love song can seem profound if it's "your song." Even "Your Song," though it beggars belief that anyone can be moved by the lyric, "If I were a sculptor - but then again no." These songs are designed to be banal, so that anyone who hears them at the right moment can impose their own emotions over the top and give them a cod-profundity. With the right lighting and the proper amount of wine, "Girl On TV" by the Lyte Funky Ones could resonate.

Truly great love songs don't need to find the mood; they set the mood. Great love songs capture some truth about love that really expresses the author's experience, and, with any luck, reflects on the listener's experience as well. Even if the listener is single, bitter and drunk. Well, especially if he's drunk.

Real love songs have something more interesting to say than, "It's a little bit funny, this feeling inside."

Songs that really say something about love, while certainly more common than songs about superheroes, are rare enough. *Comics* that really say something about love are gold dust.

Thankfully, Jen Van Meter is a soppy old romantic, and she knows how to create something spe— Something that can even touch someone like me. *Ground Zero* is a tale that reminds us all of the when we were idealists, and it finds that little spark of faith and blows on the embers to get the f— of hope flickering again. Whether you've found love or you're still looking, *Ground Zero* is a stor— reminds you that love is worth finding and worth hanging on to.

And most importantly, it reminds us that to feel love takes courage. Now, there's a million stories about love against the odds, and how it takes courage to overcome obstacles - both those imposed by the constraints of social acceptability and those imposed by the best intentions of the people who care most about us and want to see us protected. *Ground Zero* covers that ground, but it has something more to say. It tells us that the most courageous thing of all is simply to fall in love. The bravest thing to do is to place your heart in someone else's hands.

It's Zero's love story, of course, but for me the real key to the book is Twitch. If anyone knows about the courage it takes to love, it's someone who can say at such an early age that *who* they can love should not be constrained by old-fashioned concepts of normality. Twitch may have made some missteps on the road to happiness, but at least he was brave enough to take any steps at all.

I should confess, though; when it comes to Twitch, I'm terribly biased. Last year, while Jen Van Meter was still working on the book, she visited London. She and I went for dinner at Jimmy the Greek's in Soho, and over calamari and grilled halloumi, I told her how desperate I was to see greater representation of the diversity of sexuality in comics. It's a plea I've brought to the doorstep of many publishers, including some of the industry's most heavyweight carbuncles, with some apparently positive (and some not so positive) results.

In Jen's case, I was preaching to the converted, of course. In Twitch, she had already created one of the most unforced and natural gay characters in comics. Still, I told Jen that what I really wanted to see was a gay character who was not only permitted a love life, but permitted a kiss, and not only permitted a kiss, but permitted a love story.

I didn't realise quite what a receptive audience I'd found. I'm forever grateful to Jen for her heart and courage.

I should add, though, that the book's great passion and veracity isn't solely due to Jen. It boasts an impressive line-up of richly idiosyncratic artists that really make it sing with sincerity. Andi Watson, Chynna Clugston-Major, and Christine Norrie, all pop stars in the finest sense, never lose the beat as they provide their wonderful evocations of the family's romantic misadventures, while Bryan O'Malley's insolent pug-nosed faces and wide eyes provide the unmistakable refrain. There's a sense of adolescence to O'Malley's wonderful character depictions that perfectly captures the youthful flush of love. With a team like this, you're a million miles away from Celine Dion - which is a great place to be.

In closing, I should note that for two of my friends, *Hopeless Savages* really is the comics equivalent of "our song." Though friends for a while, it was over a shared love for *Hopeless Savages* that they bonded, and during a conversation about the series that one finally found the courage to ask the other out. They'll be spending Valentine's Day at the theatre, watching Sean Bean in leather pants.

I'll spend my Valentine's Day miserable and alone, thinking about Sean Bean in leather pants. That will be my sole concession to romance.

Oh, by the way, if you do get teary-eyed over Mariah Carey, it's not such a bad thing. I'll leave you with some sage advice from the Hopeless-Savages, and my favourite line from the series;

"We don't care *what* music you kids love, so long as you *have* music to love."

Andrew Wheeler
London, 12th February 2003

Andrew Wheeler is a professional entertainment journalist and editor of Ninth Art [www.ninthart.com] the comics journalism website for the discerning reader. GWM with GSH, he enjoys pina coladas and taking walks in the rain...

chapter 1

THE HOPELESS-SAVAGE FAMILY

Dirk Hopeless
a.k.a. David Sterling

Nikki Savage

Rat Bastard
Hopeless-Savage

Arsenal Fierce
Hopeless-Savage

Twitch Strummer
Hopeless-Savage

Skank Zero
Hopeless Savage

EXTENDED FAMILY

Norwegian "Weej" Blue
The family's long-time manager

Dusted Bunnies - Zero's band

Emma, bass

Toby, guitar

Flora, drums

...*NOTES* ON THE EXPERIMENT. *YOU* CAN WORK WITH MISTER KINCAID.

SORRY TO SPEED BUMP YOU. I'M ZERO.

I KNOW WHO YOU ARE.

YOU CAN *COPY* THAT. I'LL LET YOU KNOW HOW IT COMES *OUT.*

SAYS HERE YOUR FIRST NAME'S *GINGER.* FOR REAL?

YEAH. AFTER THE DRUMMER? GINGER BAKER?

CREAM. SWERVAL.

SO WE COOK OFF THE CARBON *DIOXIDE,* THEN TITRATE THE *PRODUCT* TO ITS *EQUIVALENCE* POINT?

YEAH...

WHAT?

NOTHING. JUST... YOU MUST'VE DONE THE *READING.*

YEAH...?

YOUR *TYPE* DOESN'T OFTEN *BOTHER. THAT'S* ALL.

THING ABOUT YER MUM, LUV...

...IS SHE STARTED OUT ALL *SWEET*, LIKE.

YER Ꭻ CUDDLEBUG Ꭻ

WHOLESOME, Y'MIGHT SAY.

Y'ARE LIKE SHE WERE... TALENTED, DECENT...

...HARDLY A *SPOT* OF TROUBLE...

SAVAGE'S BAKERY

...MOSTWISE...

...AND ONE DAY YER MUM JUS' WENT OFF.

THE LAD WERE HER MEANS OF ESCAPE, RIGHT?

EAST

AN' HE TOOK HER SINGIN' SERIOUS...

...HELPED HER FIND A BAND...

...WATCHA MIGHT CALL A PERSONA...

...AND A LOT ELSE BESIDES...

...THEN SHE WERE ALONE.

OUR WEEJ DIDN'T FIND HER A DAY TOO SOON.

SO...
MUM...
THINKS...
I...?
NO.

YER MUM'S
ONLY TOLD ME
SHE SEES HER WEE
SELF MOST IN YOU.

YOU SAID
IT WASN'T
HIS FAULT! I'M
NOT A BAKER'S
DAUGHTER FROM
NEBRASKA!

SHE CAN'T
BELIEVE A SQUALLING
MOVIE DATE WILL
RUIN ME!

CAN
SHE?

DA MAY
BE OFF BASE,
ZERO. IT MAY NOT
ALL BE ABOUT
YOU.

THE FAME'N'SHAME CREW'S 'ERE SOON...

...THERE'S THIS "BEST OF" RELEASE WITH THE OLD SONGS...

...NOW 'ER BABY WANTS TO GROW UP ON 'ER...

...RIGHT WHEN SHE'S DREDGIN' UP THE PAST AND FEELIN' ALL AGED.

YER BROTHER MAY BE RIGHT.

I'LL TALK TO YER MUM ABOUT THE DATING BAN.

BUT YER GROUNDED FOR TWO WEEKS ANYWISE, AN' ON LEGITIMATE TERMS.

SO DON'T BE SULKING ABOUT IT ALL OVER THE PLACE, RIGHT?

YESSIR.

OFF TO YER ROOM, THEN. YOU'LL BE CALLED FER DINNER.

...LAME, BUT WE COULD GO ON AN OLD-FASHIONED *DATE* SOMETIME...

KEEP *"HOKEY."* IT'S *AWFUL* BUT CONVEYS A *SHRED* OF *PERSONALITY.*

NOW GET THE SQUALL *OFF* MY *LOCKER* OR YOU'RE WEARING IT *HOME.*

ZED? *WAIT* A SEC AND I'LL GIVE YOU A *LIFT.*

NAH. HAVE A GOOD WEEKEND, FLORA.

...SO *THEN* THERE'S A *HUGE* CRASH AND *EVERYONE* AT THE PARTY COMES *RUSHING* INTO THE *KITCHEN* AND THE *TABLE* IS IN *PIECES* ON THE *FLOOR*...

YOU GONNA *EAT* THIS? I'M *STARVING.*

...*IN* HIS BOXERS, ON HIS ASS, *RIGHT* ON TOP OF THE *TABLE* MESS.

HE'S *TRYING* TO PULL ON HIS *SWEATER* BUT IT'S *STUCK* SO HE CAN'T *SEE*...

...EXCEPT *blah blah blah SISTER,* WHO'S *FREAKING blah blah blah TABLE,* AND *I'M blah blah blah PANTRY, IN* MY SKIMPIEST...

...*PLAUSIBLE* DENIABILITY SO *LONG* AS *NO* ONE RECOGNIZES MY *SHOE*...

YOU SHOVE OVER...

MAKE ME.

HEY, *GUYS?* WHAT'S THE *SWOO* ON GINGER *KINCAID?*

HE WAS THE KLUTZ IN THE HALL *FRIDAY.* NOT VERY *EPT* SOCIALLY.

SO... *HE'S* LOOKING FOR HIS *PANTS* BUT *I'VE* GOT THEM...

*SUPER-*GENIUS LONER. HE *SMELLED* WEIRD ALL THROUGH SIXTH GRADE.

I SEE HIM EVERY *WEDNESDAY* AT COMIX COMET. *SHY.* I *THINK* HE'S A BIG *GAMER,* TOO.

WHY?

NO REASON.

IN THE *PANTRY* IN YOUR *PANTIES* WITH HIS *PANTS?* WE'VE *GOT* TO USE THAT IN A *SONG*...

HEY.

HEY.

SO. THAT WAS ON *PURPOSE* ON FRIDAY.

THAT WHAT?

YOU KNOCKED ME DOWN ON *PURPOSE.*

SO I WOULDN'T HAVE TO HEAR *HIM* WITH THAT OTHER *GIRL.*

IT WAS AN *ACCIDENT.* I *SAID* SORRY.

I'M *TRYING* TO *THANK* YOU FOR LOOKING *OUT* FOR ME. IT WAS *NICE.*

CAN WE GET TO *WORK,* PLEASE? THERE'S A *LOT* TO DO.

RIGHT. *ANYWAY,* ONCE I'M NOT *GROUNDED,* DO YOU WANT TO--

THANK YOU, BUT *NO.*

WHAT THE *SQUALL?* YOU *DON'T* EVEN KNOW--

PLEASE LIMIT DISCUSSION TO *CLASSWORK,* MISS HOPELESS-SAVAGE.

IS YOUR PREPARATION *READY?*

YES, SIR.

HERE YOU GO THEN. CARRY ON.

NO, YOU DON'T EVEN KNOW WHAT I WAS GOING TO SAY.

WERE YOU GOING TO SUGGEST WE SEE A MOVIE OR SOMETHING LIKE THAT?

"NO BIG THING, JUST FRIENDS HANGING OUT"?

YES, BUT I... WHAT DO YOU--

LOOK. I KNOW THIS ONE AND I DON'T WANT IT. I'VE GOT TO STAY FOCUSED ON SCHOOL.

WHA'?

I DON'T WANT YOUR HEAD ON MY SHOULDER WHILE YOU TELL ME WHAT A GREAT FRIEND I AM, SO SENSITIVE, JUST LIKE A BROTHER.

I DON'T WANT TO HAVE TO ACT HAPPY FOR YOU WHEN YOU GO OFF WITH SOME CHARISMATIC IDIOT WHO-- AT BEST-- THINKS YOU ARE AN ORDINARY GIRL...

I DON'T WANT TO BE THE NICE GUY YOU HANG OUT WITH WHILE YOU REPAIR THE DAMAGE DONE TO YOUR SELF-IMAGE BY EGOTISTICAL THUGS WHO WILDLY UNDERESTIMATE YOUR WORTH.

...AND NOT THE TREASURE I KNOW YOU TO BE.

I DON'T WANT TO LOOK AT YOU WISTFULLY EVERY SO OFTEN, BUT NEVER DARE ADMIT I'VE BEEN WILD ABOUT YOU SINCE FIRST GRADE BECAUSE IT WOULD COMPLICATE YOUR LIFE AND RUIN THE FRIENDSHIP.

I'VE SEEN IT. I DON'T WANT IT. SORRY.

OH, CRAP.

"SO THAT'S WHAT WAS GRINDING ME..."

ART
AMATEUR ROCK TELEVIS!

SKANK ZERO? YOU GO BY ZERO, RIGHT?

LISTEN, *GOT A MINUTE?* I WANTED TO GET SOME *IDEAS* FOR YOUR *SPOTS.*

CAN YOU TELL ME A LITTLE ABOUT YOUR LIFE?

MY LIFE?

LESSEE. GINGER KINCAID, THE *HOOSKIEST,* SMARTEST GUY I'VE *EVER* MET *HATES* ME BECAUSE HE *LOVES* ME AND ALSO BECAUSE IT'S *MY* FAULT NOW THAT OUR *CHEMISTRY* EXPERIMENT BLEW UP.

I'VE RUINED MUM'S *FAVORITE* SWEATER.

OH, AND I'M *GROUNDED.*

MY LIFE IS AN EMBARASSINGLY *PEDESTRIAN* TEENAGE *CESSPOOL.*

THAT'S *GREAT.*

CUT IT, PAUL.

THINK WE COULD GO TO *SCHOOL* WITH YOU, TALK TO THIS *GINGER* KID?

chapter 2

YOU DID *ALL* THIS *JUST* SO...

...THEY COULDN'T *AIR* YOU TALKING ABOUT LIKING A *BOY*?

FESSING TO IT ON A *DUBIOUS* CABLE ROXPOSE...

IF I'M PASHED FOR *GINGER*, IT'S BETWEEN *US*.

AND GETTING *ARRESTED*?

THINK *THAT'LL* IMPRESS THIS GUY? YOUR *PARENTS*?

AND IT'S LESS *ROMANTIC* THAN A WEEPING *ABSCESS*.

'SIDES KID, WE ALREADY *UPLOADED* THAT STUFF. EDITING LAB GOT IT AT *SIX*.

...MAKES IT LOOK LIKE I'M GONE ON THE *MELODRAMA*, NOT *HIM*.

IT AIRS IN, *WHAT*, LANCE, *SIX* WEEKS?

YOU DON'T *HAVE* TO *USE* THAT STUFF. *PLEASE*--

YOU *KIDDING*? IT'S A *GREAT* BIT. IRONIC, SELF-AWARE, *SHARP*.

TELL YOU WHAT. *COOPERATE* 'TIL WE'RE DONE *TAPING* AND...

...I WON'T PRESS CHARGES, RAT YOU OUT TO THE *FOLKS*, OR AIR *THIS*.

AND HEY. YOU GET IT *RIGHT* WITH THIS KID, HE WON'T *CARE* ABOUT MY SHOW. *TRUST* ME.

"SO I HAD A LITTLE OVER A **MONTH** TO IRRELEVATE **WHATEVER** THEY SHOWED ON FAME 'N' SHAME..."

"...NOTHING BUT LANCE'S **GOOD WILL** KEEPING THE NIGHT'S STUNT **QUIET**, AND, DON'T FORGET, I'M **STILL...**"

...**GROUNDED!** I'VE BEEN WORRIED **SICK!** IT'S THAT **THAD!** YOU--

MUM, **NO.** I **JUST** WENT FOR A SQUALLING **WALK.**

I DON'T CARE IF YOU WERE **RESCUING** DROWNING ORPHAN **NUNS!**

IS THAT **CONCURRENT** OR **CONSECUTIVE?** PER MY **ALREADY** GROUNDEDNESS?

YOU **SNUCK** OUT, SCARED ME **HALF** TO DEATH, AND YOU'RE **SO** GROUNDED--

DON'T YOU **SASS** ME, YOUNG LADY! I'VE HAD **JUST** ABOUT ENOUGH--

CAN YOU **HEAR** YOURSELF? MUM, WHAT'S **HAPPENED** TO YOU?

...TALK HER **DOWN,** DAD. IT'S **NOT** ALL ME. **SHE'S** GONE SQUIRRELLY.

I **CAN'T** TALK TO HER. SHE'S TURNING ME INTO **MY** MOTHER. **YOU** DO IT, DIRK.

...WITHOUT *THACO* IS ALL. HOW'D YOU GET THE *AREA* FOR THE *FUNCTION?*

UH, GINGER?

EVALUATE THE INTEGRAL FROM *ZERO* TO *PI.* AND DON'T BE *IDIOTIC.* YOU'RE PRIVILEGING *STATS* OVER *STORY.*

REALITY IS FOR PEOPLE WHO CAN'T HAND' FAN'

ORDERING RANDOMNESS *IS* STORY... WAIT, HOW'D YOU GET THE *INTEGRAL?*

SUBSTITUTE *X* FOR THE PARENTHETICAL VALUE AND *DX* FOR THE *DIFFERENTIAL.*

GINGER? UM-- ZERO...

YEAH, ALEX, *ZERO.* TO *PI.*

THE *CHARACTER* IS THE STORY, DAVE. STATS ARE JUST A *CONTRACT* BE--

YOU *SURE?* I DON'T THINK THAT'S *RIGHT...*

GINGER!

HE'S RIGHT. *DIFFERENTIATE* IT AGAIN, YOU'LL *SEE.*

WHA--?! OH. *YOU.* WHAT DO YOU *WANT?*

I... I WAS GOING TO *ASK...*

DIRECTIONS? THE *COOL* KIDS SIT OVER *THERE.*

UNLESS YOU WERE *LOOKING* FOR SOMEONE TO MAKE *FUN* OF?

...NEVER MIND.

WAIT...

...to wear on blurrish days?

Looks good.

Why come you're not getting school kit?

I've already got my uniforms. An--

We're going next door.

Catch up?

Skankabelle? Wanna go to the Comet?

You never let me touch anything in there.

I wanna try more stuff on.

Tell you what. You can pay when you're done...

...then come straight next door, okay?

Swerval.

I'm a curly durrish my turban

PINK furrish

sniffle

What happened?

My glasses. They--unh...

...threw my glasses in there.

Let's get my sibs 'n' chase 'em!

I'd run into a wall.

HOP!

COMICS COMET

Careful, 'Kay? These things're full of surprises.

DOLLAR-A-POUND

Skankabelle!

Zeeeeerooooo!

Zero Hopeless-Savage!

Over here! In the alley!

...control my brain. Then oh oh oh oh oh

Then the ba ba bas

Got 'em! I got 'em!

Know why people say 'eureka'?

'cuz you reek after digging in the trash for something?

Oi. These them?

Yes.

Good. Let's get home.

Where you live, kid? We'll walk you.

THAT *WAS* GINGER... BUT...

...I DON'T REMEMBER *EVER* SEEING HIM *AFTER* THAT.

WHY WOULD HE NEVER SAY HI *LATER?* WAS I TOO *RAFFISH?* WHAT?

GUESS YOU'LL HAVE TO *ASK* HIM.

ASK HIM? ASK HIM *HOW? WHY?*

WHAT IF HE--

DOESN'T GIVE YOU THE ANSWER YOU *WANT?*

SORT THINGS WITH *MUM,* OKAY?

HARDER THAN IT *LOOKS,* ISN'T IT?

RIGHT. *LANCE* TOLD ME ABOUT YOUR *CANDID CAMERA* MOMENTS.

I'VE *PERSUADED* HIM NOT TO USE *ANY* OF IT. BUT YOU *OWE* US.

OKAY IF I *SIT* HERE?

IT'S A *NOMINALLY* FREE COUNTRY.

WHAT DID I *DO?* WHY ARE *YOU...?*

MY *GRADES* HAVE DROPPED.

MISTER BING IS *PISSED* AT ME ABOUT THE STUFF IN *CHEMISTRY.*

I *NEED* HIS RECOMMENDATION FOR *MIT.*

YOU'RE SAYING THAT'S *MINE?* I OWN YOUR *GRADES* NOW?

NO. IT'S JUST... I'M *TRYING* FOR EARLY ADMISSION, AND I DON'T *DARE* GET INTO TROUBLE AT *SCHOOL.*

AND *YOU...* ARE... TROUBLE.

FOR *ME,* ANYWAY.

KINCAI

chapter 3

...AWFUL?

NAH. 'S *BOLLOCKS*. JUS' *WATCH* 'IM AN' *DON*' BITE. FER *ZERO*, YEH?

"PARENTS ALL *GRATTERED* AT ME."

"STUPID *PARENTS*."

...TERNATIONALLY RANKED MARTIAL *ARTIST*. BY AGE *TWELVE*, YOU HAD PUT FOUR KIDS IN THE *HOSPITAL* AND HAD BEEN *EXPELLED* FROM *TEN* SCHOOLS.

YOUR *FOLKS* HAVE *SPOTTY* PASTS. DID THEY... *SYMPATHIZE*?

AND *SOMEHOW* YOU AVOIDED A JUVENILE *RECORD*.

WITH *ME*, OR THE KIDS I *INJURED*?

I WAS NEVER *CHARGED* BECAUSE IN *EVERY* CASE I WAS *PROTECTING* A *SMALLER* KID, EVEN IF I GOT CARRIED *AWAY* A BIT...

...*MUM* AN' *DA* APPRECIATED THE *MOTIVE*, BUT *HATED* THE METHOD.

BEATING BASTARDS *DOWN* RARELY *STOPS* THEM BEING BASTARDS, Y'SEE?

THEY WERE *RIGHT*. SO I FOUND *OTHER* USES FOR MY... *TALENT*.

RIGHT. WELL, *YEAH*. OKAY...

THAT ANOTHER CLAUDE SHI *ORIGINAL* YOU'RE WEARING...?

MUM AND DA *HIDING* FROM *LANCE*?

OUT TO *DINNER*. THEY'VE *DONE* THEIR SHARE. CAN'T BEAR THE *SIGHT* OF 'IM.

TWITCH'LL BE DONE SOON. FETCH *ZERO*?

"I'M A *MESS*.

"OVER A *STUPID BOY*."

...*OLD* WERE YOU? WHEN YOU CAME *OUT*?

DON'T KNOW THAT I EVER *REALLY* DID. NOT LIKE *THAT*.

IT WAS PRETTY *OBVIOUS*, I THINK. THE *CLOTHES*, THE *MUSIC*...

...*THEY* PROBABLY KNEW I WAS A *MOD* BEFORE *I* DID.

AND THEY'VE NEVER BEEN *ANYTHING BUT* LOVING AND *SUPPORTIVE*.

THAT'S, UM, NOT *EXACTLY* WHAT--

RIGHT. I'M *SURE* THEY'D *ASSUMED* I'D BE *PUNK* LIKE THEM...

...BUT THEY'RE *VERY* OPEN, ACCEPTING PEOPLE.

THEY *ALWAYS* SAID, "WE DON'T CARE *WHAT* MUSIC YOU KIDS *LOVE*, SO LONG AS YOU *HAVE* MUSIC TO LOVE."

BUT *SERIOUSLY*, LANCE. DIDN'T *YOU* SAY YOUR *VIEWERS* COULDN'T *HANDLE* ME TALKING ABOUT BEING *QUEER*?

...ON ABOUT HOW HE DIDN'T WANT *ME* "GETTING POLITICAL," THEN--

WE *SHOULDN'T* HAVE LET HIM *PROVOKE* US. I'M *SORRY,* SKANKABELLE.

DON'T *WORRY* ABOUT IT. *REALLY.*

THAT *PARTICULAR* EMBARASSMENT IS NOW A *SPECK.*

DO *YOU* GUYS EVEN KNOW *WHY* I'M *REGROUNDED?*

I WENT TO HIS *HOUSE* FRIDAY NIGHT...

...JUST A *MISUNDER-STANDING.* DID YOU *EVEN*--

CALM *DOWN,* RAY. SHE'S NOT *DONE* WITH THE... WITH HER *EXCUSE.*

YOU WERE *SAYING,* ZERO, THAT YOU FELT *DISCOURAGED?* HUMILIATED?

PULPED. I MEAN, IT *LOOKED* LIKE *GINGER* AND SOME *OTHER* GUY...

...WERE *LAUGHING* AT ME.

YER *DOWN* THERE, IN THE *RAIN,* SINGIN' TO 'IM, AND HE *LAUGHS?*

OF ALL THE... *I* WOULD HAVE GIVEN M' *LEFT*--

IT'S *NOT* AS IF IT WAS A *GOOD* SONG.

I WAS SPONTANIZING *AND* OUT OF TUNE.

THAT'S NOT THE *POINT.* HE'S *CLEARLY* AN IDIOT. YOU CAN DO *BETTER.*

...BUT I **DON'T** THINK YOU'LL **LIKE** IT.

...JUILLIARD! I CAN'T **BELIEVE** IT!

I **KNEW** THEY'D **TAKE** YOU...

SHI

...HOW COULD THEY **NOT?**

LET'S GO CHECK AT **YOUR** HOUSE. IF I GOT **MINE--**

ALREADY **HEARD.** I HAVEN'T "DEMONSTRATED SUFFICIENT **FOCUS**" ON ACTING.

I'M GOING TO HAVE TO STAY **LOCAL.** BEST **ART** DEPARTMENT.

THEN **I'LL** STAY **TOO.** I WANT US TO BE **TOGETHER.**

IF HE'S THE **ONE,** AND **YOU'RE** THE ONE FOR **HIM,** HE'LL **KNOW...**

...WANTS *ME* IN THE *POETRY* SEMINAR NEXT SEMESTER.

'S *GREAT.*

THE CHANGINGMAN

ARE YOU EVEN *LISTENING*? IT'S *SCHEDULED* OPPOSITE *PLAYWRITING.*

SO *PICK* ONE.

...*GOT* TO CALL MY *FOLKS!* THIS IS *GREAT.*

YEAH? YOU CHECK OUT THIS *REHEARSAL* SCHEDULE?

I'M *NOT* UP FOR *TEN* WEEKS OF DANCING *ALONE.*

IT'S *BEEN FUN.*

COFF
TEAS · CA

TRIBUNE
CHS STUDENT TAKES ISSAC STERN PRIZE

HE'LL KNOW YOU *CARE* ABOUT HIS PROBLEMS *AND* HIS *ACCOMPLISHMENTS.*

...STILL UPSET OVER A LITTLE FLING?

I'M NOT UPSET. I'M BUSY.

...TOO BUSY TO EVEN TALK LIKE I'M A PERSON.

WHAT DOES THAT MEAN? IF YOU DIDN'T ALWAYS NEED TO...

...FEEL LIKE HELL. SOME BIRTHDAY, HUNH?

DON'T COMPLAIN TO ME. YOU INSISTED ON GOING OUT.

...AND YOU CARRIED ON LIKE A SPOILED BRAT.

BUT YOU'RE NEVER MEAN OR SPITEFUL. NOT YOU.

"PAUL WELLER"

THE CHANGINGMAN

HE'LL KNOW HE'S HAPPIER WITH YOU THAN WITHOUT.

HE'LL KNOW *YOU* AREN'T THINKING ABOUT *ANYONE ELSE.*

IF I KNEW ANYTHING *TRULY* HELPFUL, I'D STILL BE WITH *HENRY*. SORRY.

OH, TWITCH...

THIS *YER* CLAUDE'S *BROTHER* WE'RE TALKING ABOUT?

YEAH.

GIVE HIM SOME *TIME*. HELP WITH THE WASHING UP.

...*ALL* TWISTED UP INS-- HEY.

I THINK YOU WERE *BRAVE*. LIKE THAT *THING*? ABOUT IF YOU *LOVE* SOMEONE--

SET 'EM *FREE*? PASSIVE-AGGRESSIVE *CRAP'S* WHAT *THAT* IS.

TERRY
DODSON

chapter 4

ZERO, *WAIT!*

DON'T, SON. JUST LET HER *GO.*

WHAT?

TO *CLASS.* ZERO'S IN A *LOT* OF *TROUBLE,* AND...

AND SHE *NEEDS* TO KEEP HER MIND ON HER *OBLIGATIONS.* AS DO *YOU.*

IF YOU *MUST* SPEAK WITH HER, DO SO *OUTSIDE* OF SCHOOL HOURS.

BUT... *BUT* SHE'S...

...STILL *GROUNDED?*

OH, *THEY* KNOW. AND WE CAN'T *EXCHANGE* AT *SCHOOL.*

IT'S PART OF THE *DEAL.*

...*KNOW* HE WAS *GOING* TO USE *THAT!*

...FAMILY *TRADITION* OF *MUSICAL* INTEREST...

...OTHER *BUNNIES'*LL BE *WATCHING*, RIGHT?

HOW'D HE GET *HOLD* OF *THAT?*

...*AND* OF *REBELLION*...

...*KIDS* WERE SO *CUTE!*

...*SCHOOL* HAD BEEN *BURYING* ASSAULT *REPORTS*...

...*ELDEST* DAUGHTER, *ARSENAL*, TURNING HER TASTE FOR *VIOLENCE* TO...

GIT MAKES IT *SOUND* AS IF *YER DOIN'* THE *ASSAULTIN'*.

TWITCH! HENRY! THEY'RE SHOWING *PRIDE NINETY-SIX!*

...*YOUNGEST SON, TWITCH, POLITICALLY* ACTIVE AT AN *EARLY*...

HENRY'S HERE? I DIDN'T KNOW *HENRY* WAS HERE...

THE
END

Bios

JEN VAN METER made her comic book debut alongside Buffy the Vampire Slayer, scripting that character's first-ever comic book story for the *Dark Horse Presents Annual 1998*. She followed it up with a collaboration with Frank Quitely in Vertigo's horror anthology *Flinch*, a script for DC's *Gotham Knights*, a segment of Marvel's *Captain America #50*, and the licensed comic book tie-in *The Blair Witch Project*, the best-selling single issue in Oni Press' history. *Hopeless Savages* is her first creator-owned work (if you don't count her son, Elliot), and its first series was nominated for an Eisner in 2002. Her most recent releases include a *Batman* Elseworlds book for DC called *Golden Streets of Gotham*, the third chronicle of the Hopeless-Savage family, *Too Much Hopeless Savages!*, and a second child.

BRYAN O'MALLEY is from Canada and in addition to his handling art chores here, he has inked an issue of *Queen & Country* and letters *Blue Monday, Jason and the Argobots* and a variety of other things. Bryan's own *Lost at Sea* appeared in the *Oni Color Special 2002* and will be an original graphic novel from Oni in 2003. He also created the comic strip *Style*, which has run at onipress.com. And as if that wasn't enough, one can always find more from Bryan on the internet at radiomaru.com.

Born in West Germany, CHRISTINE NORRIE has lived many places but fondly claims St.Louis as her hometown, the place she grew to love comic books. She moved to New York in the late nineties, worked in the business end of comic book publishing for DC Comics, and later became a freelance illustrator. Since the debut of the first *Hopeless Savages* series, she's been nominated for many awards including the prestigious Eisner Award, the Russ Manning Award, and was a recipient for the New York City Comic Book Museum's Award for Breakout Artist of 2002. Christine Norrie is the comic artist for *Redbook* magazine's *Q&A with John Gray: You and Him* and *Spy Kids* for Disney, and just published her first graphic novel, *Cheat*. She is currently at work on the next *Hopeless Savages* series and another, slightly cheerier, romance for Oni Press. She resides in the historic North Shore of Staten Island with her husband and their parakeet, rabbit, three cats, and the ever-marvelous dog, Orwell. She was joined on *Ground Zero* by her sister, CATHERINE NORRIE, who previously has worked in graphic design. This is Catherine's first comic book work.

ANDI WATSON is the creator of *Skeleton Key, Geisha, Slow News Day, Dumped,* and *Breakfast After Noon*. He also scripted the *Buffy the Vampire Slayer* comics for two years, has optioned *Skeleton Key* for a cartoon series, designed animated advent calendars for AOL.co.uk, and had one of his cover images appear fleetingly in the background of teen flick *Coyote Ugly*. In the year 2001, Andi and *Breakfast After Noon* were nominated for an Eisner Award for Best Limited Series, the second nomination for the artist (he previously received notice for the collection of *Geisha* in 2000). He is currently hard at work on a brand-new series, *Love Fights*, for Oni Press, who are also releasing an expanded edition of *Geisha*. Despite his brushes with fame, he remains remarkably down to earth.

CHYNNA CLUGSTON-MAJOR is the talented cartoonist behind the award-nominated series, *Blue Monday*—available in two trade paper backs, *The Kids are Alright* and *Absolute Beginners*, and a series of holiday-themed one-shots that will be collected into the book *Inbetween Days* in the fall of 2003. She has also done work for Dark Horse's *Buffy the Vampire Slayer* comics, Paul Dini's *Jingle Belle*, and Marvel's *Ultimate Marvel Team-Up*. When not drawing, she is usually shouting at neighborhood children from her studio window or cooking up the best tacos known to man. Her next project is *Scooter Girl,* a six-issue miniseries scheduled for release from Oni Press in May 2003.

Acknowledgments

Jen thanks:

The artists who made this book possible; Terry's covers, the flashback art by Andi, Christine and Chynna, and the amazing work of Bryan O'Malley all make me so proud of and for this story. Jamie, Joe and James at Oni Press, for making it happen and for their dear friendship. Steve Woodcock for his help with the chem. and calc. homework. As always, my friends and family, who make it all possible, most especially Greg and Elliot.

Bryan thanks:

I'd like to dedicate my work on this book to Jen, Christine, Chynna, Andi, Jamie, Joe, James, Kelley, Keith, and all the other cool people that made it all happen. I had a lot of fun and I hope we can still be friends. Extra special thanks to Christopher Butcher for putting up with me during this period. I was inconsolable. He also helped on the book, I think; I can't remember. I was on drugs.

Jamie thanks:

Andrew Wheeler for helping us put our best foot forward; Catherine Norrie for bailing us out; Andy Greenwald and Kieron Gillen for opening up their address books; and Marie Du Santiago for her sartorial splendor and kindness.

✱✱✱✱✱✱✱✱✱✱✱✱✱✱✱✱✱✱✱✱✱✱✱✱

********* sketches and things **********

Thumbnails and character sketches by Bryan Lee O'Malley.

Original pencils for chapter 2 by Christine Norrie.

Zero by Matthew Clark.

Arsenal by Ross Campbell.